Based on the TV series *SpongeBob SquarePants*® created by Stephen Hillenburg as seen on Nickelodeon®

SIMON SPOTLIGHT
An imprint of Simon & Schuster Children's Publishing Division
1230 Avenue of the Americas, New York, New York 10020

Manufactured in the United States of America
Abridged Edition
ISBN 1-4169-0989-3

Go, Graduate!

All the Best from Bikini Bottom

by David Lewman

Simon Spotlight/Nickelodeon
New York London Toronto Sydney

YOU DID IT!
You're ready . . . TO GRADUATE!

You read all the right books!
Jelly Fishing
Jelly Fishing

You
really
kept it
together!

Sure,
maybe you got behind once or twice,

BUT YOU DID IT!

Great job, pardner!
Graduatin' can be tougher than wrestlin' a giant clam!

Big deal. I went to college.

TIPS FOR THE BIG DAY

First things first:

You'll want to be very clean for graduation.

You'll
want to
get
dressed
up.

And please go to the bathroom
before
the ceremony.

Arr . . . don't be
afraid to walk up and
get your diploma!

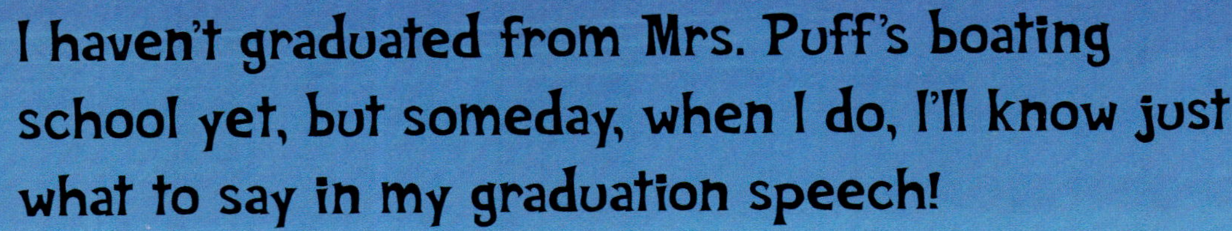

I haven't graduated from Mrs. Puff's boating school yet, but someday, when I do, I'll know just what to say in my graduation speech!

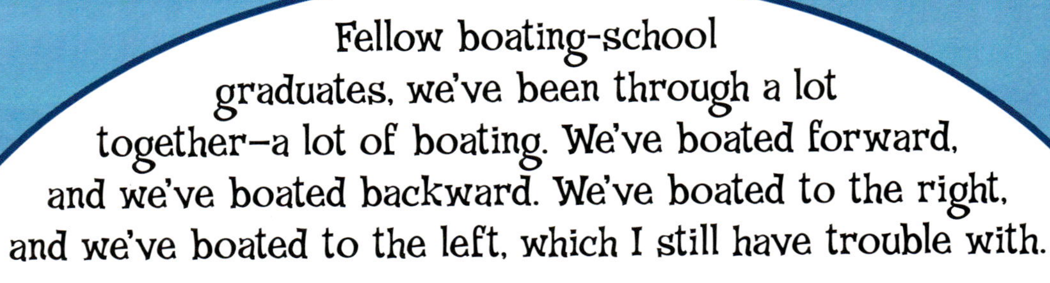

Fellow boating-school graduates, we've been through a lot together—a lot of boating. We've boated forward, and we've boated backward. We've boated to the right, and we've boated to the left, which I still have trouble with.

But thanks to the greatest boating teacher in the world, Mrs. Puff, we've learned how to boat with the best of boaters . . . boatily.

So let me just say in conclusion that

I'M READY . . . TO DRIVE A BOAT!

Come on, fellow boaters, let's get out there and boat!

Thank you.

THE BEST PART OF GRADUATING:

THE CELEBRATION!

You'll figure out the best way to celebrate your graduation, because you're a deep thinker.

After all, you've
got a great
brain!

You've worked hard, graduate.
How about a party? With live music, of course!

And as we say at
the Krusty Krab,
every party needs
a patty.

With so many possibilities and choices to make, you may feel like you are having a hard time standing on two feet.

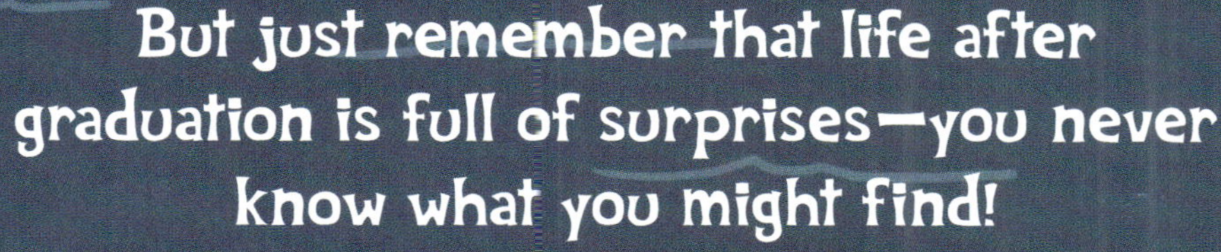

But just remember that life after graduation is full of surprises—you never know what you might find!

Maybe someday you'll be . . .

a doctor . . .
EXHIBIT A
or maybe a lawyer.

Maybe you'll own a business
and make boatloads of money!

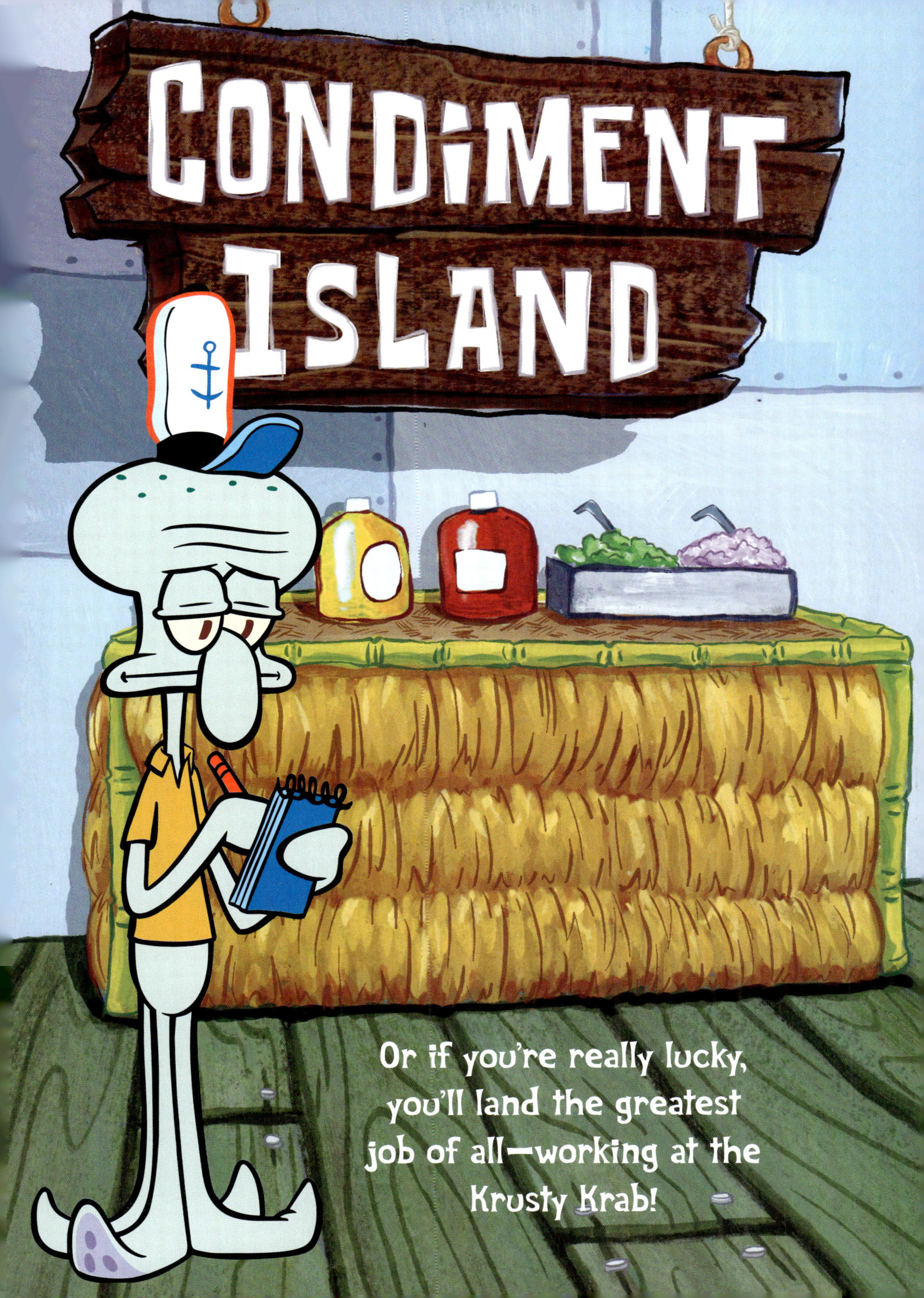

Or if you're really lucky, you'll land the greatest job of all—working at the Krusty Krab!

GRADUATE, I SALUTE YOU.

Go have some fun. And remember,
no matter what you decide to do next . . .

you're sure to be a

star.